Disciples Devoted to Fellowship

The One Another Principle

A Bible Study Workbook by

Matthew Allen

© 2023 Spiritbuilding Publishers.
All rights reserved. No part of this book may be reproduced in any form without the written permission of the publisher.

Published by
Spiritbuilding Publishers
9700 Ferry Road, Waynesville, Ohio 45068

DISCIPLES DEVOTED TO FELLOWSHIP
The One Another Principle
By Matthew Allen

ISBN: 978-1955285-70-4

Scripture quotations are from the ESV® Bible (The Holy Bible, English Standard Version®), Copyright © 2001 by Crossway Bibles, a publishing ministry of Good News Publishers. Used by permission. All rights reserved.

Spiritbuilding
PUBLISHERS

spiritbuilding.com

Table of Contents

Introduction 1

Lesson 1   Lifting Up One Another 2

Lesson 2   Exhorting One Another 7

Lesson 3   Confessing Our Faults to One Another 12

Lesson 4   Praying for One Another 19

Lesson 5   Rejoicing for One Another 23

Lesson 6   Weeping with One Another 27

Lesson 7   Growing with One Another 32

Lesson 8   Sharing with One Another 38

Lesson 9   Trusting One Another 44

Lesson 10 Bearing with One Another 50

Lesson 11 Forgiving One Another 55

Lesson 12 Submitting to One Another 59

Lesson 13 Loving One Another 63

Introduction

And they devoted themselves to the apostles' teaching and the fellowship, to the breaking of bread and the prayers. And awe came upon every soul, and many wonders and signs were being done through the apostles. And all who believed were together and had all things in common. And they were selling their possessions and belongings and distributing the proceeds to all, as any had need. And day by day, attending the temple together and breaking bread in their homes, they received their food with glad and generous hearts, praising God and having favor with all the people. And the Lord added to their number day by day those who were being saved, Acts 2.42–47.

Perhaps there is no better passage that describes the life of the earliest Christians. Their life consisted of:

- a sense of awe and heartfelt unity.
- selling their belongings and taking care of the needs of others.
- assembling together daily.
- breaking bread together at home, with generous hearts.
- praising God.
- having favor with all the people.

For them, Christianity was much more than a once-a-week occurrence. It enveloped every aspect of life. It *was* life! American Christianity struggles with this. We are busy, rich, overworked, and often distracted, which can make us push our spiritual pursuits down the priority list to a mere subsection of life, rather than them *being our life*. With all the pressure of American culture, it is not surprising to see brothers and sisters disconnected from and relating superficially to the rest of their spiritual family.

How can we correct this tendency?

In *Disciples Devoted to Fellowship*, we intend to reinforce these objectives:

- a yearning to be together.
- the development of a servant's heart.

I'm excited you have joined me in this challenging study. To God be the glory!

Matthew Allen

June 2023

Lesson 1
Lifting Up One Another
Defining Fellowship

With what is *fellowship* most connected within today's religious world? If you said *food and fun*, you'd be correct. I would suggest to you that this is not a proper connotation of the word. Eating together and enjoying the company of others is a result of what we are seeking to define.

Fellowship is synonymous with these words: *partnership; communion; contribution; joint participation; companionship; sharing; partakers.*[1] Another reference defines *fellowship* in the following way: *Close association involving mutual interests and sharing, association, communion, fellowship, close relationship.*[2] What do these examinations teach? Each member of the local church is to have a personal and emotional connection with the work that is being conducted and with others inside the congregation who are participating in its various works.

What share do you have in the work of your congregation? Is it just being present at worship services, Bible studies, and making your financial contribution? What kind of fellowship do you have with your congregation in its:

- teaching program? (children or adult)
- evangelistic outreach?
- encouragement of members?
- visitation of one another?
- service to widows and widowers?
- mentorship and encouragement of its youth?

Fellowship is NOT just being at church. It is engaging in partnership with your brothers and sisters in the church. Are you a **spectator** or a **participant**?

A Look at Epaphroditus

Epaphroditus provides Bible students with a great example of *fellowship*. He is identified as a Christian sent by the Philippians to help Paul during a time of need, Philippians 2.25; 4.18.

Understanding who Epaphroditus was, is best understood by seeing him inside his relationship to Paul and the Philippians. Paul uses three significant terms in 2.25 to characterize his bond with him:

- "My brother"—He was one in the faith with Paul.
- "My fellow worker"—He was a colleague of Paul in evangelizing.
- "My fellow soldier"—He struggled side by side with Paul against adversaries of the gospel. *This military metaphor suggests that Epaphroditus experienced suffering and conflict in his ministry.*[3]

Epaphroditus (in the case of the context of Philippians) served as a minister to Paul's material needs by bringing him monetary gifts the Philippian church entrusted him with. Notice how Paul describes these gifts in 4.18:

- "A fragrant offering"
- "A sacrifice acceptable and pleasing to God"

Epaphroditus completed his mission. Note 2.30: *for he nearly died for the work of Christ, risking his life to complete what was lacking in your service to me.* Look again at 4.18. What did receipt of these gifts do for Paul? *I have received full payment,* **and more. I am well supplied ...**

Thinking about Paul's situation ...

In Philippians 1.12–14, Paul identifies his circumstances and conditions. He was imprisoned. Despite the poor situation, he chose to rejoice, 1.18; 2.17. As you read parts of chapter 4, where Paul focuses on the supplies/money that Epaphroditus brought to him, it is easy to see how he had been uplifted by the actions of the Philippian church. And, not only that, but he had also had the company of Epaphroditus. Having others around during dark times can be a huge source of encouragement.

Lifting Up One Another: How Do We Do it?

Therefore encourage one another and build one another up, just as you are doing, 1 Thessalonians 5.11.

What does this look like?

Esteem others higher. Christians esteem others higher than themselves, Philippians 2.3–4. Have high regards, great respect, and favorable thoughts of the people in your circle of trust and influence. Expect the best from your brothers and sisters.

Be wise in your speech. Communicate more effectively by thinking before you speak. If there is a word that is more appropriate in a conversation, use it. Start with a praise. Never confront others. Instead, point out on how both of you can make things better. Speak at the same level as your audience, giving them due respect. There's no need to come in with an authoritarian voice to get your message heard.

Be encouraging. Encouragement is an expression and assurance of one's hope and future in words, presence, and sincerity.

Be quick to forgive. When others make a mistake, be quick to forgive and forget; releasing them from guilt and shame that may take root in one's heart when not dealt with over time. See Colossians 3.12–14.

Be understanding. Wisdom and understanding go hand in hand. Understanding starts by being an active listener (not planning a reply as one is speaking), asking intelligent questions to gain further insight, and being accepting of what the speaker is sharing. Then, answer without condemning. Or don't answer at all and decide to just be a listening ear.

Zero gossip. Keep others' secrets. Never speak stuff that causes unnecessary hurt to others by speaking unclaimed rumors behind their back.

Share knowledge. Found an article or book that's useful? Share it with your friends. Sharing knowledge helps us learn, discover, and understand things that are interesting. They have immediate application for better results in our work and life. They edify our soul and improve our daily conversations.

Stay humble. Humility and maturity are synonymous. A dignified person accomplishes much, but brags little. They are secure in their standing without needing to make noise, often treating everyone with tremendous respect, regardless of position.

Be positive! Positive thinking goes beyond having the drive and motivation for personal success. Positive thinking is explicit, definite, and outspoken. It's contagious. Build up your loved ones with your positiveness, allowing them to be open for better things to come.

Love. *Love is patient, love is kind. It does not envy, it does not boast, it is not proud. It is not rude, it is not self-seeking, it is not easily angered, it keeps no record of wrongs. Love does not delight in evil but rejoices with the truth. It always protects, always trusts, always hopes, always perseveres. Love never fails … And now these three remain: faith, hope, and love. But the greatest of these is love,* 1 Corinthians 13, NIV. Care for your loved ones how you would want to be cared for. Build up one another how you would like to be inspired.[4]

For Thought and Reflection

1. What is the most common connotation for *fellowship* in today's religious world? Does this connect with how the word is used in the New Testament? Explain.

2. What does *fellowship* mean, when speaking of how it is used in the New Testament?

3. How is Epaphroditus a great example of *fellowship* in action?

4. In what ways had he uplifted Paul?

5. What was Paul's situation as he wrote the letter to the Philippians?

6. Why is *building up* or *uplifting* others so important?

7. When examining ten things that can help build up others, why do you think we start with *respect*? How much respect do you see in the society around us?

8. How can improving one's communication skills help in the uplifting of others?

9. Why can gossip be so discouraging?

10. Why is positive thinking and positive attitude so important?

11. Besides 1 Corinthians 13, can you think of any other passages that instruct us on putting love in action?

12. How has today's lesson helped you as you think about the relationships inside our congregation?

13. What are some things you can do this week to uplift others within the spiritual family you are part of?

Lesson 2
Exhorting One Another
Introduction

One of our greatest challenges may be to view our spiritual family in the special way Scripture calls for. Referring to your congregation as a *family* is not just a catchphrase. It should be a growing reality inside your life in every sense of the word. You are not alone in your journey to heaven. If you've been blessed to have physical family that are Christians, that's great. But along with them, you have God's family—made up of people with different experiences, maturity levels, personalities, and talents. All of these make up the group of people that will journey with you to the goal—eternal life with God in heaven.

It is important to see the spiritual family for the blessing that it is. And it is equally important that to understand the great need to be a part of it by serving, encouraging, and exhorting others. Those who limit their interaction with the family will limit their potential for spiritual growth. They will also neglect the admonition in Hebrews 10.24 that instructs Christians to *consider how to stir up one another to love and good works.*

This lesson focuses on *exhorting one another.* Perhaps the first place we think of this is 2 Timothy 4.2: *Preach the word; be ready in season and out of season; reprove, rebuke, and exhort, with complete patience and teaching.*

Exhort carries along the idea of encouragement, but with the idea of some force behind it. We don't use the word *exhortation* very much today but when you were little and heading out the door on a freezing cold day, maybe your mother made an exhortation for you to put on your hat and zip up your coat! Exhortation is to urge by a strong, often stirring argument, admonition, advice, or appeal.[5]

Parakaleō

This is the Greek word for *exhort* in 2 Timothy 4.2. Here are some general definitions for this word:

- To ask to come and be present where the speaker is, *call to one's side.*
- To urge strongly, *appeal to, urge, encourage.*
- Impress upon someone.

- To make a strong request for something, request, implore, entreat.
- To instill someone with courage or cheer, comfort, encourage, cheer up.[6]

The way the word should be used is determined by the context. In the 2 Timothy context, the word is associated with "admonishment," "encouragement of those who obey," "appealing to," and *telling them what they ought to do*.[7] In other places, the same word is translated "urge," such as in 1 Timothy 1.3; 2.1; 4.13; and 6.2.[8] The word was also used in military contexts for the encouragement of soldiers.[9]

Going back to our text, Paul moves from the negative to the positive in explaining the role of the preacher. To *reprove* someone involves giving them reason to understand that something is wrong in their life. To *rebuke* someone is to convict them that they have done that thing. The word *exhort* is transitional in that Paul is moving out of the negative to the positive which is *patience* and *teaching*. The preacher confronts their sin and then encourages them out of it. He comes alongside after having confronted them to encourage them to take the steps to change.[10]

How is it done?

The simple answer is found in 1 Thessalonians 2.11–12: *For you know how,* **like a father with his children,** *we exhorted each one of you and encouraged you and charged you to walk in a manner worthy of God, who calls you into his own kingdom and glory.* Think how a father plays an important role with his children, leading and guiding them, and correcting them. The idea is that the exhortation is done with a spirit of love, care, and concern.

Glen Pease in his writing on *The Gift of Exhortation,* points out that the first four letters of the Greek word for "exhort" are *para,* from which we get parallel lines that run alongside each other. He says, "the true exhorter is one who does not rub you the wrong way because he is not trying to cross you, but to run parallel with you."[11] This is the person that comes along side us to be a comfort and companion. Even if this person has to communicate that you are wrong, they do so in love and out of concern. Their goal is to help and encourage you to be your best.

It has been said that *a person has made a step toward genuine maturity when he or she realizes the greatest gift they can provide others consists in being a radiant and encouraging person.*[12] Obtaining this gift can certainly be a challenge. There may be times where we tend to be judgmental, and our advice will turn people off. Edward Steichen became one of the world's greatest photographers because his mother was an encourager. When Edward took his first pictures, only 1 out of 50 were half-way decent. His father told him to put away the camera and try another hobby. That was his exhortation, but his mother took another approach. She said that the one picture of his sister at the piano more than made up for the other 49. She encouraged him to try again and not let failure stop him. *Her encouragement was the beginning of the climb to the top.* "History is filled with examples of how one person's encouraging word or action motivates another to press on to victory."[13]

You can help someone advance in their walk with God

Read Exodus 18.1–24. Here we are introduced to Jethro, Moses' father-in-law. One of Moses' jobs was to judge the people in disputes and other matters. Note specifically 18.13: *The next day Moses sat to judge the people, and the people stood around Moses from morning till evening.*

Now, carefully read 18.14–17 and see how Jethro exhorted Moses. *What you are doing is not good,* 18.17. Then, note the angle that he approaches Moses with. It is not with a spirit of condemnation or charging him with ignorance, but from genuine concern: *You and the people with you will certainly wear yourselves out, for the thing is too heavy for you. You are not able to do it alone,* 18.18. As you read the remaining verses, Jethro advises Moses to set up a court system. This exhortation not only helped Moses, but it helped everyone in Israel.

Those who are gifted in exhortation **do not just judge what is wrong, but they also have a helpful answer as to how to set it right.** *The gifted exhorter can give counsel that moves people to actions that solve problems.* This is the person who helps:

- turn words into action.
- prayers be answered.
- vision move toward accomplishment.

Conclusion

It takes work and plenty of forethought and prayer to be an exhorter. It is not something that a person can rush into with little thought. There needs to be a plan and a purpose. Words need to be carefully chosen. The timing needs to be right. Assurances need to be given that failure doesn't have to be the end. We can all become better exhorters and encouragers. Are you willing to do the work it takes to do this effectively?

For Thought and Reflection

1. Read Hebrews 10.24. What is the goal behind stirring up others? How effective are you in this work?

2. Reread the definitions for exhort that are listed on pages 7–8. What definition do you think best fits the context of 2 Timothy 4.2?

3. Think of a time when you received exhortation. What are your feelings toward the person who came alongside you to help? How can you use that experience to further your own methods of exhortation?

4. How does 1 Thessalonians 2.11–12 help us to understand how exhortation is to be given?

5. How strongly do you value the companionship of others in your spiritual walk? How does it fit inside the area of exhortation?

6. Why is it so important to be defined as an encouraging person?

7. How has the encouragement of someone else helped you go to the next level of spiritual living? Where would you be without it? Explain.

8. What lessons can we learn about Jethro's exhortation to Moses?

9. What type of planning needs to be given before we decide to exhort someone:

    a. In our attitude toward the other person:

    b. In understanding the problem they're confronting:

    c. In the words we choose:

    d. In the solutions we provide:

10. Why is timing an important consideration as we think about how to exhort someone?

11. How can today's lesson help you head toward spiritual maturity?

Lesson 3

Confessing Our Faults to One Another

Introduction

This lesson will focus on James 5.7–20. Verses 13–18 have been sources of confusion to many Christians. What exactly is James referring to? Is the *sickness* mentioned in these verses physical or spiritual, or both? What is involved in the *confession* in 5.16?

How much do I have to reveal, and to whom shall I confess it?

What role does prayer play in all of this?

Understanding the Context of James

James is one of the earliest epistles. In the decade before, Jewish Christians had been subjected to great persecution and dispersed around Palestine to avoid mistreatment and death by Jewish authorities. The Christians were under great stress and having trouble. Some were in outright physical persecution.

Notice how James urges his readers to:

- Move with patience during trials, 1.1–4.
- Stay faithful by remaining steadfast and look ahead to the *crown of life*, 1.12.
- Keep focused on the spiritual, trusting in the guiding hand of God, 1.17–18.
- Avoid being angry with the world, becoming bitter and vengeful, 1.20–21.
- Act on their faith, 2.14–26.
- Put away selfishness and jealousy, 3.13–18.
- Reject worldliness, 4.1—5.6.

Next, just before the section we focus on in this lesson, James revisits the theme that he opened the epistle with:

> Be patient, therefore, brothers, until the coming of the Lord. See how the farmer waits for the precious fruit of the earth, being patient about it, until it receives

the early and the late rains. You also, be patient. Establish your hearts, for the coming of the Lord is at hand. Do not grumble against one another, brothers, so that you may not be judged; behold, the Judge is standing at the door. As an example of suffering and patience, brothers, take the prophets who spoke in the name of the Lord. Behold, we consider those blessed who remained steadfast. You have heard of the steadfastness of Job, and you have seen the purpose of the Lord, how the Lord is compassionate and merciful, James 5:7–11.

How could we summarize this? James wants his readers to stand and remain faithful amid great persecution. Focus on the word *establish* in 5.8 (*strengthen* NASB). In the original language this word means to "prop up your heart with determination, persistence, and inner strength." It involves the concept of hanging on without complaint.

The Key for Endurance

Now, please reread 5.13–18. What is the emphasis? Can you see it? It's **prayer.** *Pray* or *prayer* is used in every verse between v. 14–18:

- *Let him **pray**, 5.14.*
- *And the **prayer** of the faith will save the one who is sick…5.15.*
- *Confess your sins and **pray** for one another that you may be healed…5.16.*
- *Elijah… **prayed** fervently that it might not rain…5.17.*
- *Then he **prayed** again, and heaven gave rain…5.18.*

Does the *sickness* refer to a physical condition, or does it seem to apply much more to the **spiritual soul that is suffering?** I think the answer is easy to see. James is thinking about people who are struggling spiritually, to the point of exhaustion, and need to learn to **depend on divine resources.**

Notice how we can organize these verses into compact units, with different areas of focus:

VERSES	THEME	FOCUSES ON
5.13	Prayer and Comfort	The **believer** who is weak and struggling.
5.14–15	Prayer and Restoration	The **shepherds** who minister to the wounded believer who is weary, depressed, and defeated.

| 5.16a | Prayer and Fellowship | The **congregation** who stands with and encourages the person who is struggling. |
| 5.16b–18 | Prayer and Power | **God** and His ability to hear and answer the prayer of the righteous. |

Why can we be so confident of this referring mainly to those who are struggling with a spiritual problem verses physical sickness and disease?

When James mentions a *sick* person in 5.14, the wording means *to be sick and, as a result, in a state of weakness and incapacity.*[14] In the New Testament, this word is used mostly to represent being weak in the faith.[15] I believe this passage is about healing spiritual weakness, weariness, exhaustion, and depression which calls for a spiritual solution: prayer. To assert that this is referring to physical healing doesn't seem to fit the context well and is hard to reconcile with the last two verses of the chapter. Therefore, a section on how to help people who are spiritually weak and broken seems to make more sense.

James 5.13—Prayer and Comfort

Is anyone among you suffering? Let him pray, James 5.13a. Look at 5.10, where the exact same word is used. The word involves suffering evil treatment or persecution. If there are those in the church enduring those things, the idea is to turn to God in prayer. This is addressing the person who is experiencing deep spiritual pain. It is suffering mentally and emotionally from the effects of their trials, temptations, and persecutions.

Is anyone cheerful? Let him sing praise, James 5.13b. This is in the text to compare or contrast to the first sentence. James is referring to a person's spirit: a suffering soul and/or wounded broken spirit vs. a happy soul and/or a rejoicing spirit. One sings, the other pleads. Both are for comfort. Praise is a fundamental component in spiritual comfort. Prayer is basic to spiritual comfort.

James 5.14–15—Prayer and Restoration

Is anyone among you sick? Let him call for the elders of the church, and let them pray over him, anointing him with oil in the name of the Lord, James 5.14. This is the person who has hit bottom. They've been defeated. Picture them lying on the spiritual battlefield. It's hard to pray. It's hard to make progress on your own. So, what is James' instruction? Call the elders of the church to come alongside you. They're spiritually strong. They have the spiritual strength you need. They're godly and you should draw on their strength. Think about how these fit in with Paul's teaching in Galatians 6.1.

How should the elders respond to a spiritually defeated person? They are to pray over him and anoint him with oil in the name of the Lord. This is no ceremonial oiling. In the New Testament, the Greek word used here always refers to "secular usage where you literally oil something." In the ancient Middle East, oil and wine were often used as topical applications to cleanse wounds and soothe the skin. According to Luke 7.46, *if you went to a home and you were the main guest, the first thing they might do after they cleaned your feet was pour oil on your head, a fragrant lovely oil just to soothe you from the dirt and the dust and the heat of the day. In that part of the world, the sun could dry you out and it was a refreshing time.*[16]

Oiling someone could have a literal and a metaphorical sense. If a Christian were literally being beaten and persecuted, the elders could take out some oil and rub the skin of the believer. But metaphorically, it could be referring to the stimulation and encouragement of a person's spirit, whose heart needs to be warmed and strength provided to their weakness. Think of a soldier who has been in the field. They're dry and parched from battle, nearing exhaustion. Wounds are all over them. They're weak and weary and tired of fighting the spiritual battle. Now, they have been able to come to their commanders—their shepherds—who come alongside and pray with them, sharing their spiritual strength. See their compassion and strength being used to bind up the broken heart.

This is the job of our shepherds. This is the ministry of restoration. See Psalm 23.

Notice 5.15a. The idea is that those who are exhausted and weary receive spiritual restoration and strength. *The prayer of faith will save the one who is sick.* The idea is that the faithful prayer of the shepherds can deliver or rescue a person. This is all so a person can be lifted by the Lord. Raise him up carries the idea of "rebuilding, to arise, to awaken, or to excite."[17]

Now, 5.15b. Not only will God raise up this spiritually defeated person, but He will also forgive their sin. The promise is full restoration. Any sins that pulled him to weakness will be forgiven. Any sins that he fell prey to after succumbing to weakness will be forgiven. During this time, some Christians would have become weak from persecution. They would have compounded that weakness through sin.

James 5.16a—Prayer and Fellowship

Therefore, confess your sins to one another and pray for one another, that you may be healed. Now, James turns his attention to the congregation. The admonition is not to wait until you get to the bottom but maintain a relationship with other believers—so that you are always praying for one another.

One of the general elements of fellowship is **mutual honesty.** And that means we must confess our sins to one another. That is, *we do not hide our weaknesses.* Sin wants you alone. It wants you isolated. If sin is private or secret, you can nurse it, nurture it, and feed it. God wants it open and exposed among the people who love you. To confess means to let it out; be honest; share your struggles; and let people know you're in a battle. Why? *So, you won't become weak, defeated, weary, exhausted, wounded, or victimized by Satan.*

Who is the *one another* in 5.16a? Simply put, it is *other believers in your circle.*[18] Other believers don't have to know every specific detail of every sin, but they should know about the weaknesses of your life until God gives you the victory over those areas. The idea is to share your life so that you may be healed or experience spiritual restoration. *Tell someone where your battle is and then pray for the battles they are fighting.*

James 5.16b–18—Prayer and Power

The prayer of a righteous person has great power as it is working, James 5.16b. The *power* in this verse is defined as energy. So, the energetic, empowered prayer of a righteous person will have a tremendous impact.

Elijah is used as an illustration. First, James says Elijah was just like us. He was human and subject to fleshly passions. He had times of great spiritual strength, followed by times of incredible spiritual weakness. But he *prayed fervently.* That means he really prayed. As a result, God literally controlled the rain because of his prayer.

If we keep using the spiritual metaphor found in these verses, just as God sent refreshing rain down on a dry, parched land in response to Elijah's powerful prayer, so God can provide blessing, joy, and refreshment to a parched, dry, weary and exhausted soul that is in desperate need.

Conclusion

To me, looking at James 5.13–18 from a spiritual sickness point of view makes much more sense than what may be considered as the traditional view. It solves the problem of deciding if elders should literally apply oil to a physically sick person as they pray over them. It helps us understand the role of prayer in spiritual endurance. And it helps us understand the ministry of restoration that falls to the shepherds who oversee a local congregation.

May we all humble ourselves and see the value and purpose of confessing sin to other people. We need help and encouragement during times of great spiritual need after Satan has had his way with us. We need to see the extreme value of our relationships with each other. Not every person in the congregation needs to know everything about our life, our struggles, and weaknesses, but *someone* needs to know. Find those you feel comfortable sharing with and lean on them, along with God, for spiritual strength and advice. You'll be glad you did.

For Thought and Reflection

1. What is the most typical interpretation of James 5.13–18? Does it refer to physical sickness or spiritual sickness?

2. How does understanding the overall context of the epistle of James help you better understand this section?

3. Who is the person in view in 5.13? What type of suffering is he most likely facing?

4. Who is in focus in 5.14–15? What are they to do in helping the one who has come to them?

5. What is a primary role and function of the eldership? How does 5.14–15 reinforce this concept?

6. What does the word *save* mean in 5.15a?

7. How sure is the forgiveness in 5.15b?

8. What is involved in confession in 5.16a? How well do you follow through on instructions in this passage?

9. What makes a righteous person's prayer so powerful?

10. What can we learn about Elijah and prayer in 5.16b–18?

11. How has today's lesson helped you in your study on discipleship?

Lesson 4

Praying for One Another

Introduction

It has been said that if one only knew of all the good accomplished and the evil averted through prayer, he or she would be even more diligent in their prayers.[19] We can be assured that when we pray, God listens. The following passages attest to how prayer works:

> If any of you lacks wisdom, let him ask God, who gives generously to all without reproach, and it will be given him. But let him ask in faith, with no doubting, for the one who doubts is like a wave of the sea that is driven and tossed by the wind. For that person must not suppose that he will receive anything from the Lord, James 1:5–7.

> Draw near to God, and he will draw near to you. Cleanse your hands, you sinners, and purify your hearts, you double-minded, James 4:8.

> Therefore, confess your sins to one another and pray for one another, that you may be healed. The prayer of a righteous person has great power as it is working. Elijah was a man with a nature like ours, and he prayed fervently that it might not rain, and for three years and six months it did not rain on the earth. Then he prayed again, and heaven gave rain, and the earth bore its fruit, James 5:16–18.

When life throws out problems, trials, temptations, and setbacks, we need to be reminded that God hears and will answer our prayers.

Prayer Works for the Christian

Jesus testified to the power and effectiveness of prayer. See Matthew 7.7–11. This passage teaches us that God will supply all our needs—giving what is good to those who ask. Paul certainly believed in the power of prayer: "Now to him who is able to do far more abundantly than all that we ask or think, according to the power at work within us," (Ephesians 3:20). We also can consider the instructions:

> Rejoice in the Lord always; again I will say, rejoice. Let your reasonableness be known to everyone. The Lord is at hand; do not be anxious about anything, but in everything by prayer and supplication with thanksgiving let your requests be made known to God. And the peace of God, which surpasses all understanding, will guard your hearts and your minds in Christ Jesus, Philippians 4:4–7.

There is nothing which pertains to body, mind, estate, friends, conflicts, losses, trials, hopes, fears, in which we may not go and spread it all out before the Lord.[20]

It was the Hebrew writer who said we may draw near to God *in confidence*, Hebrews 4.16. See also Hebrews 10.22–23 and 11.6. The message behind these passages is that prayer must be conducted in faith—trusting in the assurances of God to answer it.

Notice James 5.16b again: *The prayer of a righteous person has great power as it is working.* What exactly does this mean? Effective prayers are those that are sincere, earnest, hearty, and persevering. This is opposed to listless or indifferent prayer that can be cold and lifeless. It's not about a repetition of the same old phrases and common sayings, but **a sincere heart that trusts in the leading of our heavenly Father who loves his children**.

Praying for Others

What are some things for which we can pray for one another?

The spiritual growth of our brothers and sisters

Paul often prayed for his brethren—and requested their prayer for him. See passages like 1 Thessalonians 5.25; 2 Thessalonians 3.1; and Hebrews 13.18–19. We should also be specific as we pray about these things.

- Philippians 1.9–10—Paul prayed for the **spiritual growth** of the Philippians.
- Ephesians 6.19—Paul prayed for **boldness** in his preaching.
- Colossians 4.3—Paul prayed that **doors of opportunity** would be opened for him.
- Romans 15.30–31—Paul requested the Romans pray for his **deliverance from *unbelievers* in *Judea*,** and that his ***service for Jerusalem may be acceptable*** to the saints.

Perhaps the greatest example in learning how to pray for others is seen here:

> "For this reason I bow my knees before the Father, from whom every family in heaven and on earth is named, that according to the riches of his glory he may grant you to be strengthened with power through his Spirit in your inner being, so that Christ may dwell in your hearts through faith—that you, being rooted and grounded in love," Ephesians 3:14–17.

Just take that reading apart. We can pray for:

- the spiritual strength of one another, 3.16.
- each other to be *rooted and grounded in love*, 3.17.
- each other to be *filled with the fullness of God,* 3.18–19.

If you know of someone in the family spiritually struggling, pray for them specifically. And, let them know how much you care by telling them you are praying for them.

Temporal Needs

See Matthew 6.11. *Daily bread* refers to the simple necessities of life: food, shelter, clothing, health, etc. Notice, we're instructed to pray for these things—even if God knows we need them. This suggests that we must learn to depend on God for our material needs, which helps us worry less, Matthew 6.25–32. What temporal needs do your brothers and sisters have that you could pray for?

Deliverance from Temptation

Temptation is real. See Matthew 6.13. We can pray for other people specifically if we know what temptations they are facing. We can pray that they'll have the strength to withstand. Passages like 1 Corinthians 10.13 also help as they remind us that in every temptation God will provide a way of escape!

For Thought and Reflection

1. How do the passages in the epistle of James help you as you consider the power and effectiveness of prayer?

2. Think back to some of your recent prayers. How has God answered these? Do you have an example you can share with the class?

3. How does Jesus' teaching in Matthew 7.7–11 help you in your daily spiritual walk? What is Jesus NOT talking about in this passage?

4. How does prayer produce peace? (Philippians 4.6–7)

5. What do the Hebrew passages mentioned in this lesson teach us concerning the effectiveness of our prayer?

6. What is a good definition of an *effective* prayer? See James 5.16b–18.

7. What good can come by praying for the spiritual growth of your brothers/sisters? What good can come for you?

8. What are some temporal needs some of your closest brothers and sisters have? How are you praying for those needs to be met?

9. What is the key to being able to pray for specific temptations others have? How can we develop more confidence to share these types of things with each other?

10. How does it make you feel when you know others in your spiritual family are praying specifically for you? How can you apply this in your prayers?

11. How has today's lesson helped you in your study on discipleship?

Lesson 5

Rejoicing for One Another

Introduction

In Paul's writings to the churches at Rome and Corinth, two passages stand out:

> *If one member suffers, all suffer together; if one member is honored, all rejoice together,* 1 Corinthians 12.26.

> *Rejoice with those who rejoice, weep with those who weep,* Romans 12.15.

From Paul's writings, we learn Christians should have a unique care for one another. When we discuss fellowship, there is a certain inherent unity and togetherness. Following through on what is written in these two passages provides powerful evidence of our fellowship together.

What does it mean to rejoice together?

A Look at the Context of Romans 12

Romans 12 begins the application section of the book. While the first 11 chapters are mostly doctrinal, looking at the basis of our salvation and the assurance of it, the final 5 demonstrate the result of that salvation: a changed life.

The following goal might further our understanding of who and what Paul is focusing on in verses 9–21:

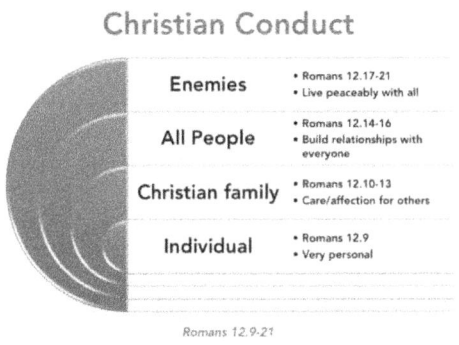

Romans 12.9-21

Romans 12.9 is speaking to the individual Christian. Practical Christian living begins with simple priorities:

- Honest love, 12.9a
- Hating evil, 12.9b
- A commitment to what is right, 12.9c

In Romans 12.10–13, the focus widens to the Christian family. We are each called to:

- Love one another with brotherly affection, 12.10a.
- Seek, above all, to honor other Christians, rather than be honored yourself, 12.10b.
- Serve others with enthusiastic, whole-hearted, zealous, obedient, and diligent care, 12.11.
- Endure trials, our own **and** the trials of others. During those things we are to rejoice, be patient, and be constant in prayer, 12.12.
- See to the needs of others, 12.13.

In Romans 12.14–16—we look outside the body and think of all people. These verses challenge us on how we live in relationship to every person. In 12.14, Paul begins with the worst of people: *those who persecute you.* How should we respond? *With a blessing.* Again, this is a general statement. *Anyone who persecutes you, you bless.* This teaching is distinctively Christian. The world does not respond to mistreatment or persecution with love. But here, we are instructed to "pursue the one who treats us with evil intentions with the intent of doing honor with blessing."

Finally, in Romans 12.17–21—the focus goes all the way to our enemies. We are to always maintain our honor, 12.17; *live peaceably with all,* 12.18; and to never avenge ourselves, 12.19–20. This is all so we can overcome evil, not be overcome by it.

Rejoicing with those who Rejoice

In explaining the context, I purposely left out comments on 12.15–16. Now that we understand the background and Paul's purpose behind these writings, we'll look at these two verses in depth.

Rejoice with those who rejoice, weep with those who weep.

This is the natural result of true love and humility. It is the application of loving like Jesus. It is not always easy to get in touch with the emotions of others. Inherent in 12.15 are the concepts of:

- **Compassion** which means *suffering with*.
- **Empathy** which is *the ability to identify with and experience the feelings and dispositions of others.*[21]

When we rejoice with others, we are sharing in their joys, triumphs, and successes. This can be a challenge. For example, when we see others succeed where we have failed, it can lead to envy, jealousy, and resentment. So, to follow through on what Paul is calling for in this verse, it requires the total absence of these things. MacArthur says that it is distinctively Christian to rejoice at someone else's prosperity.[22] Think about it this way: *What do the worldly do?* **Whoever mocks the poor insults his Maker; he who is glad at calamity will not go unpunished**, Proverbs 17.5.

How do we accomplish this?

The key is found in 12.16: *live in harmony with each other.* The NASB says, *be of the same mind toward each other.* The admonition is to think about everyone the same. Later in Romans Paul would write: *May the God of endurance and encouragement grant you to live in such harmony with one another, in accord with Christ Jesus,* Romans 15.5. Think also of the teaching found in Philippians 1.27 and 2.2–4.

When Paul wrote 1 Corinthians 1.10, the emphasis was not focused as much on doctrinal correctness as as it was with eliminating social cliques and social strata. Christians are to *be united in the same mind and the same judgment.*

Now, back to our passage in 12.16. Paul gives two suggestions on how to live together in harmony:

Don't be haughty but associate with the lowly

We're not to concentrate on high things, but to associate or *be carried away with* that which is lowly.[23] This doesn't mean that we never associate with those who are high up—it's just that we don't pursue high status or concentrate on "high" things.

Never be wise in your own sight

In other words, don't be satisfied that everything begins and ends with you. *Lean not on your own understanding,* Proverbs 3.5.

For Thought and Reflection

1. When you read Romans 12.15 and 1 Corinthians 12.26, how do these verses effect you? Do you feel you are doing a good job presently in applying these passages?

2. If not, what is holding you back?

3. How does understanding the context of 12.9–21 help you in better understanding Romans 12.15?

4. How are compassion and empathy defined?

5. How does empathy play a role in fulfilling the rejoicing in 12.15?

6. How can your old self get in the way of fulfilling Romans 12.15?

7. What does it mean to live in harmony with one another?

Lesson 6

Weeping with One Another

Introduction

Previously we examined the first half of Romans 12.15: *Rejoice with those who rejoice, weep with those who weep.*

We learned how this is the application of loving like Jesus. *It is not always easy to get in touch with the feelings of others.* Inside Romans 12.15 are the concepts of compassion, which means *suffering with*, and empathy which is *the ability to identify with and experience the feelings and dispositions of others.*

When compared with the *rejoicing* that is mentioned in the first part of the verse, the *weeping* may appear to be easier. But it does require deliberate effort. It is not always easy for us to involve ourselves in the distress of others. But throughout both Old and New Testament periods, it is something that God's people have been called upon to do.

Why This Can be Difficult

It is easy to be indifferent to the troubles and sorrows of others, especially when we are dealing with our own. Our mind might say, *I have enough of my own problems, why get involved with someone else's?* Or, *I can barely cope with my situation, how could I possibly offer something of value to someone else?*

Also, we need to guard against the tendency to gloat when people's sufferings are the result of their own carelessness and sin. We must resist the urge to say, "they get what they deserve."

Job's Friends

Job's trouble came upon him suddenly and with no expectation. Not only did he lose all his material possessions and offspring (Job 1), he lost his health (Job 2.1–10). Upon hearing this, Eliphaz, Bildad, and Zophar came to comfort him. We read:

> Now when Job's three friends heard of all this evil that had come upon him, they came each from his own place, Eliphaz the Temanite, Bildad the Shuhite, and Zophar the Naamathite. They made an appointment together to come to show him sympathy and comfort him. And when they saw him from a distance, they did not recognize him. And they raised their voices and wept, and they tore their robes and sprinkled dust on their heads toward heaven. And they sat with him on the ground seven days and seven nights, and no one spoke a word to him, for they saw that his suffering was very great, Job 2.11–13.

What is said here is very moving. Just read the words slowly and let them sink in:

Job's condition was so bad, *they did not recognize him.*

His suffering was *very great.*

When they saw him, Eliphaz, Bildad, and Zophar *raised their voices and wept, and they tore their robes and sprinkled dust on their heads…*

They *sat with Job on the ground, …and no one spoke a word to him.*

Sometimes, all you can do is be there. The grief is so overwhelming, astonishing, and stupefying, that no words are adequate. In these situations, there is a *reverential awe* with which we approach the sufferer and a *tender caution* with which we address them.[24] It is almost as if any words spoken would be out of place.

Other Biblical Examples

Two additional examples stand out where Biblical characters exhibited deep and tender compassion toward others who were not necessarily fellow followers of God. One is in Psalm 35.13–14: *But I, when they were sick— I wore sackcloth; I afflicted myself with fasting; I prayed with head bowed on my chest. I went about as though I grieved for my friend or my brother; as one who laments his mother, I bowed down in mourning.* Here, David is seeking God's justice against those who have aligned against him. But, notice his actions in previous times. See his empathy and compassion for others as they were struggling.

Another example is in the gospels during Jesus' teaching in Luke 10.30–37. In this case, the Samaritan man exhibited great empathy as he cared for the man who had been beaten, robbed, and left for dead on the side of the road. He made the other man's problems his own. He sacrificed his own safety, time, and resources in making sure the man received the proper care during a very difficult time.

How Empathy Benefits

The Giver

When we are empathetic toward others, it can inspire within us a sense of gratitude toward God for His personal sustaining and care as well as remind us of our total dependence on Him. It also forces us to recognize that our own personal troubles may be much lighter when compared to those around us.

The Receiver

Our care and concern take some of the weight of the sorrow away. It can serve as a balm to heal the wound suffering creates. It also can help divert their mind from only focusing on their troubles to *reciprocal affection*[25] and an attitude of gratitude to a very gracious God.

The Church

When these attitudes, care, and concern are displayed in full force and activity, the cause of Christ is greatly promoted. The beauty and excellence of Christianity is seen. Think of how those who beheld Jesus at the tomb of Lazarus were struck with his sympathy:

> When Jesus saw her weeping, and the Jews who had come with her also weeping, he was deeply moved in his spirit and greatly troubled. And he said, "Where have you laid him?" They said to him, "Lord, come and see." Jesus wept. So the Jews said, "See how he loved him!", John 11:33–36.

When persons behold Christians participating with others freely in their joys and sorrows, they too will say, "Behold how these Christians love one another; yea, and not one another only, but all around them, strangers and enemies, as well as friends!"[26] The prevalence of this disposition goes further to silence those who speak negatively about Christianity, and wins more souls, than all the arguments of doctrinal knowledge. In other words, we can speak to them in a language which they cannot but understand and feel.

Conclusion

Consider the following passages:

- *Finally, all of you, have unity of mind, sympathy, brotherly love, a tender heart, and a humble mind,* 1 Peter 3:8. We need to share the same passions. Our craving to be like our Savior and Father should imprint on us a mutuality of concern for one another because of our common fervency for God's redemptive rule. We need to stand together to survive.[27]
- *Remember those who are in prison, as though in prison with them, and those who are mistreated, since you also are in the body,"* Hebrews 13:3.
- *Let no one seek his own good, but the good of his neighbor,* 1 Corinthians 10:24.
- *If one member suffers, all suffer together; if one member is honored, all rejoice together,* 1 Corinthians 12:26.

Food for Thought and Reflection

1. Do you think weeping with those who weep can be more difficult than rejoicing with those who rejoice? Or vice-versa? Why?

2. By saying nothing initially, do you think Job's three friends did the right thing? When did they begin to make mistakes? What can we learn from this?

3. How did David treat the people around him? As you read Psalm 35, do you get the idea that he was referring to people in his immediate family, or people in general?

4. How can the Good Samaritan inspire you to be more empathetic?

5. What are some ways that empathy benefits the giver?

6. What are some ways that empathy benefits the receiver?

7. What are some ways that empathy benefits the local church?

8. What are some things you can do to grow in your empathy toward others?

9. When we help people through their problems, what does it remind us about the problems we face?

10. Where would you be today without the care and support of others who stood with you during dark times?

11. Who are some people within your spiritual family that you can be there for? What do you intend to do this week to follow through in encouraging them? Displaying the empathy that they need?

12. How have the last two lessons helped you become a better disciple of Jesus?

Lesson 7

Growing with One Another

Introduction

Reading through Acts and thinking about Luke's account of churches being established throughout Asia Minor and Europe is exciting. In these stories we see the steadfastness, perseverance, and faith of Paul and his companions. It seems they faced trouble wherever they went. Their love for Christ and His church is inspiring. These stories should also speak to us today as we think about the persons who walked away from paganism and embraced the *gospel of God*.

Imagine starting from nothing spiritually and embracing a totally different lifestyle. Imagine the reaction of your family as you began to proclaim your faith and trust for eternal salvation through a Jewish Man who was rejected by His people and ultimately crucified. Imagine your emotions and thoughts as *for the first time*, you began to experience being socially ostracized, held in suspicion, and even mistreated by other people and the governing authorities. Our first-century brothers and sisters knew firsthand what Jesus meant when he said:

> If the world hates you, know that it has hated me before it hated you. If you were of the world, the world would love you as its own; but because you are not of the world, but I chose you out of the world, therefore the world hates you. Remember the word that I said to you: 'A servant is not greater than his master.' If they persecuted me, they will also persecute you. If they kept my word, they will also keep yours. But all these things they will do to you on account of my name, because they do not know him who sent me, John 15.18–21.

All these factors would have had a great impact on the believers… *for the good*. Times of stress and pressure can drive a group of people toward unity and spiritual growth as they come together under a common cause. As we look at the New Testament church, this story repeated itself in many places. Places like Corinth, Philippi, Berea, and Ephesus come to mind. Another great example is the church in Thessalonica.

The Church in Thessalonica

Establishment

The Acts account provides details of Paul's establishing the church in this city, Acts 17.1–10. This was part of his second missionary journey. Acts 17.4 provides details of large numbers being converted: *And some of them* were persuaded and joined Paul and Silas, as did a great many of the devout Greeks and not a few of the leading women. This resulted in unbelieving Jews attempting to drive Paul and his companions from the city. They incited a mob who claimed Paul had committed crimes against the Roman empire. When they could not find Paul, they dragged Jason and a few others before the city officials. Luke provides the details:

> But the Jews were jealous, and taking some wicked men of the rabble, they formed a mob, set the city in an uproar, and attacked the house of Jason, seeking to bring them out to the crowd. And when they could not find them, they dragged Jason and some of the brothers before the city authorities, shouting, "These men who have turned the world upside down have come here also, and Jason has received them, and they are all acting against the decrees of Caesar, saying that there is another king, Jesus, Acts 17.5–7.

The city officials required Jason and the others to post a bond and then dispersed the mob. The last thing they needed was a threat to the peace and the lack of Roman intervention that the city enjoyed. Paul and Silas were sent away in the middle of the night, Acts 17.10.

Growth and Unity

A look at First and Second Thessalonians reveals how these Christians grew spiritually under difficult circumstances. They:

- Walked *in a manner worthy of God,* 1 Thessalonians 2.12; 4.1.
- Received apostolic teaching as *the word of God,* 1 Thessalonians 2.13.
- Demonstrated *faith and love,* 1 Thessalonians 3.6.
- Possessed *love for one another and for all,* 1 Thessalonians 3.12.
- Practiced *brotherly love,* 1 Thessalonians 4.9.
- Had a faith that was *growing abundantly, and the love of every one of you for one another is increasing,* 2 Thessalonians 1.3.
- Were *steadfast* and *faithful* in all the persecutions and afflictions they were enduring, 2 Thessalonians 1.4.

What We Can Learn

Spiritual growth is multi-dimensional.

Devotion to Growth

We must be committed to individual growth in the acquisition of knowledge from the word of God, remaining faithful, and possessing moral purity. We must come to view Jesus as the Lord of our life and His word as the instrument that guides our transformation. Is the word of God *at work in you,* 1 Thessalonians 2.13c?

Maturing Together

Christians mature together simultaneously with one another. In the opening verses of 1 Thessalonians, Paul mentions their *work of faith and labor of love and steadfastness of hope in our Lord Jesus Christ,* 1.3. As we work together as a spiritual family, we can draw off the energy of one another and present a strong and unified front against Satan. We are stronger together than we are individually. Simply put, we are a team. We are committed to reaching every goal *together*. This will involve help, encouragement, and exhortation—all for the purpose of spiritual growth.

Exhort one another every day, Hebrews 3.13. Why **every** day? Because the enemy attacks every day. We live in a world filled with lies. Satan's message can be conveyed subconsciously through social media, the entertainment world, and the news media. We need to be constantly saying things to one another that keep each other believing. We all need to hear how Jesus and His way is better than what the world is peddling. We need to understand that *we will die without good spiritual friends.*

Shared Experience

Christians grow stronger through shared experiences. In 1 Thessalonians 2, Paul mentions the sufferings Christians faced as they began their transition from living as a pagan to Christ.

> For you, brothers, became imitators of the churches of God in Christ Jesus that are in Judea. For you suffered the same things from your own countrymen as they did from the Jews, who killed both the Lord Jesus and the prophets, and drove us out, and displease God and oppose all mankind by hindering us from speaking to the Gentiles that they might be saved—so as always to fill up the measure of their sins, 1 Thessalonians 2.14–16.

Later, in 2 Thessalonians 1, Paul spoke of their suffering in present tense (1.5) and called on them to move forward in trust that God would *repay with affliction those who afflict you and to grant relief to you who are afflicted as well as to us,* 1.6–7a.

When we go through shared conflict and tumult, there is a certain bonding that occurs. But this doesn't just occur in negative and unpleasant circumstances. Growth also occurs when Christians share life together. There is great value in Christian families raising their kids together, traveling together, studying together, and growing old with each other. Christianity is a shared pursuit, not an individual endeavor.

What This Looks Like Locally

Collectively, the church works together in encouraging spiritual growth from the youngest to the oldest of ages:

- *Children's Bible classes.* From the youngest age, your children have a weekly opportunity to grow together through a devotional led by various brothers and sisters in the church. There is value in hearing a Bible-centered lesson and singing together.
- *Adult Bible classes* provide rich opportunities to grow in knowledge of Scripture and related topics.
- *Special occasions* where a **guest speaker** is invited to speak on a special topic or theme. The benefits of hearing biblical teaching from differing perspectives should not be dismissed.
- Regular times of *preaching, singing, and worship.* While our focus in our weekly service is on God, one of the most significant effects is our individual and collective spiritual growth.
- *Small group studies and "get-togethers."* These types of gatherings are especially effective as they tend to be less formal and often occur outside of the church building. Settings like this allow people to feel more comfortable in sharing what is going on in their life.

Individually, the local church family should be busy being part of the many differing efforts that fit inside the parameters of spiritual growth and encouragement. Men and women's retreats; teen outings; home classes; singings; potlucks; eating out together; and various "get-togethers" are important *and should be encouraged and participated in by* everyone *where applicable.* Again, these occasions ultimately center around the very spiritual purpose of encouragement, togetherness, and maintaining unity.

Spiritual growth does not only take place in a classical learning environment revolving around knowledge. It also involves building camaraderie, trust, and friendships in the social arena as well. *And all who believed were together and had all things in common. … And day by day, attending the temple together and breaking bread in their homes, they received their food with glad and generous hearts,* Acts 2.44, 46.

For Thought and Reflection

1. Think back to your start as a Christian. How important were other believers in your early growth and development? Where would you be today had you not had them in your life?

2. What do you find inspiring about the birth and establishment of the church at Thessalonica?

3. In what ways does Paul point out the spiritual growth of the Thessalonian Christians? How is this im-pressive considering the difficulties they faced?

4. What are some things you are doing to increase your commitment to personal spiritual growth?

5. What are some things you can do to exhort others every day?

6. What are some of the shared experiences you have had with others inside your local church family that has contributed to your spiritual growth?

7. How valuable to you is the spiritual family where you attend? How strong is your involvement with the family outside of the church building? How can it be improved?

8. What are some individual works you can come up with or participate in that could contribute to your own personal growth or the growth of others?

Lesson 8

Sharing with One Another
Introduction

In the first lesson, I defined fellowship, as it is used inside the New Testament. Here's a quote:

> Fellowship is synonymous with these words: *partnership; communion; contribution; joint participation; companionship; sharing; partakers*.[28] Another reference defines *fellowship* in the following way: *Close association involving mutual interests and sharing, association, communion, fellowship, close relationship*.[29] What do these examinations teach? Each member of the local church is to have a personal and emotional connection with the work that is being conducted and with others inside the congregation who are participating in its various works.

Throughout the New Testament there are many references to the sharing we have with God, Jesus, and the Spirit.

In fact, this seems to be the majority of uses. However, there are other applications, especially regarding the relationships we have with one another inside the local church family. It is these that we wish to focus on in this lesson.

Benevolent Needs

Two passages stand out: one is an example and the other a command:

> Do not neglect to do good and to share what you have, for such sacrifices are pleasing to God, Hebrews 13.16.

> By their approval of this service, they will glorify God because of your submission that comes from your confession of the gospel of Christ, and the generosity of your contribution for them and for all others, 2 Corinthians 9.13.

Another great example of sharing or *fellowship* in benevolent needs is found here:

> Now the full number of those who believed were of one heart and soul, and no one said that any of the things that belonged to him was his own, but they had everything in common. There was not a needy person among them, for as many as were owners of lands or houses sold them and brought the proceeds of what was sold and laid it at the apostles' feet, and it was distributed to each as any had need, Acts 4.32, 34–35.

When needs arise and family cannot or can no longer provide, these passages demonstrate the responsibility of the church family to rise to the occasion and help fellow brothers and sisters who are in need. When the needs of those who are in difficult situations are met, it is a prime opportunity for relationships to be strengthened. It creates strong, powerful bonds that cannot be easily broken.

The Preaching of the Gospel

In the book of Philippians, Paul uses the word *partnership* (sharing) in expressing his thankfulness for the financial contributions of that church to his ministry.[30] Reading through the epistle, it is obvious that there was a very deep level of affection between Paul and the members of the Philippian church. They believed in Paul and his work. There was a mutual trust. The communication was genuine and open. There was genuine appreciation and admiration. Both parties acted in good faith.

If we were looking for a model of the relationship between a local congregation and an evangelist, this would be a good place to start. Both parties have mutual responsibilities in making the relationship what it should be.

What an honor it is to share in the work of preaching, locally and around the world. Congregations are enriched when they make sacrifices to share in the support of evangelists. In many cases, the more a congregation decides to give, the more God blesses with additional funds. We need to trust God, just as Paul did: *And my God will supply every need of yours according to his riches in glory in Christ Jesus,* Philippians 4.19.

Suffering/Difficult Circumstances

Staying in Philippians, at the end of chapter one while teaching on congregational unity, Paul turns his attention to suffering. Chapter 1.28b–30 contains the theological explanation for suffering:

> This is a clear sign to them of their destruction, but of your salvation, and that from God. For it has been granted to you that for the sake of Christ you should not only believe in him but also suffer for his sake, engaged in the same conflict that you saw I had and now hear that I still have, Philippians 1.28b–30.

Keep in mind, Paul also was experiencing suffering for the cause of Christ (1.12–14). The Philippians were suffering. Christ also suffered. Paul writes:

> So if there is any encouragement in Christ, any comfort from love, any participation in the Spirit, any affection and sympathy, Philippians 2.1.

If Paul were communicating in modern 21st century English, the "if" in 2.1 would mean "since there is," or "because there is."[31] To better understand, we can read the passage like this:

- Since there is encouragement in Christ, ...
- Since there is comfort from love, ...

- Since there is participation in the Spirit, …
- Since there is affection and sympathy, …
- Then make my joy complete by being of the same mind…

When we experience suffering, we not only receive compassionate sympathy from deity, but also from one another. Suffering and difficult circumstances can strengthen the relationships we have with those in Christ. Here, Paul is appealing to the compassion and unity that he and they have toward each other and showing them how that can be motivation to carry out the command in Philippians 2.2. See how these concepts all work together. We have encouragement, comfort, sharing, affection and sympathy from the Father, Son, and the Spirit. But we also receive it from one another.

Lives of Devotion

In Acts 2.42 we read: *And they devoted themselves to the apostles' teaching and the fellowship, to the breaking of bread and the prayers.* Notice the components of worship that are mentioned here: teaching, communion, and prayer. This verse is probably a summary of their corporate worship on the first day of the week.

At the root of this is the sharing in a joint venture of life. Fellowship involves partnership, see Luke 5.10; Philemon 17. It is saying, "Let's do this together." In this we share with others what we have. For example, we can share encouragement. It is where we say," I have something you may need, so I want to share it with you." Hebrews 10.24–25 fits in here: "And let us consider how to stir up one another to love and good works, not neglecting to meet together, as is the habit of some, but encouraging one another, and all the more as you see the Day drawing near."

But our life of devotion is not just shared on the first day of the week in corporate worship. Acts 2.46–47 communicates daily togetherness: "And day by day, attending the temple together and breaking bread in their homes, they received their food with glad and generous hearts, praising God and having favor with all the people. And the Lord added to their number day by day those who were being saved."

What makes Christianity so attractive? *It is not just what we do on Sunday!* It is the totality of our shared life and community that speaks to the world around us. It is in our mutual relationships where we best demonstrate:

Brotherly Love

A new commandment I give to you, that you love one another: just as I have loved you, you also are to love one another. By this all people will know that you are my disciples, if you have love for one another, John 13.34–35.

The Unity Jesus Desired

I do not ask for these only, but also for those who will believe in me through their word, that they may all be one, just as you, Father, are in me, and I in you, that they also may be in us, so that the world may believe that you have sent me, John 17.20–21.

The Power of Overcoming Evil with Good:

Love one another with brotherly affection. Outdo one another in showing honor. Do not be slothful in zeal, be fervent in spirit, serve the Lord. Rejoice in hope, be patient in tribulation, be constant in prayer. Contribute to the needs of the saints and seek to show hospitality. Bless those who persecute you; bless and do not curse them. Rejoice with those who rejoice, weep with those who weep. Live in harmony with one another. Do not be haughty, but associate with the lowly. Never be wise in your own sight. Repay no one evil for evil, but give thought to do what is honorable in the sight of all. If possible, so far as it depends on you, live peaceably with all, Romans 12:10–18.

Conclusion

What a blessed life we have been called to lead! We've been given salvation. We stand in grace. We have each other. We have an advocate when we sin. We have an eternal inheritance. We have wonderful blessings of being inside a Christian family who loves, encourages, and protects us. Let's join together and build our relationships, living inside our common love.

For Thought and Reflection

1. How do we define sharing together?

2. How can the meeting of benevolent needs provide an opportunity for bonds between brethren to be strengthened? *If you have ever had your needs supplied by others, how did it make you feel?* (Think beyond financial help, etc.)

3. What would the model relationship between a congregation and the evangelist(s) it supports look like? What does Philippians teach us about this?

4. How do difficult circumstances and suffering bring brethren together?

5. Do you think of Christianity as a "joint venture of life?" What are some things you can do to grow in the ways you relate to your brothers and sisters?

6. What are some things you can do to *stir others up to love and good works?*

How will you be encouraged in this?

7. What is so powerful about the message of shared living, especially to a dark world?

Lesson 9

Trusting One Another
Introduction

Thus far we have discussed encouragement, exhortation, prayer, expressing genuine emotions, spiritual growth, and sharing with each other. It has been wonderful to explore all these concepts and this lesson should be no different. In it, we're going to get down to the core of what drives our day-to-day relationships inside the local church family: trust.

How well do you trust other individuals within the spiritual family?

Distrust breaks down relationships. It's easy to go there, especially after someone has hurt or betrayed us. In those moments, the natural thing to do is to shut down, withdraw, and build a wall around our vulnerabilities because we cannot face another round of hurt after someone does something that violates our trust.

So how do we keep from going there?

Today's lesson will look at two examples of what could be labeled as the epitome of trusting relationships. One is a look at the relationship between Paul and Timothy. The other probes the relationship between Paul and the church in Philippi. After we explore the noteworthy things from these examples, we'll get very practical and discuss ten ways you can build trust inside the relationships you have with others in your local congregation.

Two New Testament Examples
Paul and Timothy

Perhaps there is no better example of trust in action than with Paul and Timothy. The very first example where we see it expressed in written form is in Philippians 2.19–22: *I hope in the Lord Jesus to send Timothy to you soon, so that I too may be cheered by news of you.* **For I have no one like him,** *who will be genuinely concerned for your welfare. For they all seek their own interests, not those of Jesus Christ.* **But you know Timothy's proven worth, how as a son with a father he has served with me in the gospel,**" Philippians 2.19–22.

Notice how Paul expresses Timothy's high value to him as a fellow laborer in the Lord. Timothy had proven himself repeatedly as someone who was reliable, trustworthy, and sincere. When Paul was personally unable to see what was going on inside local churches, he saw that Timothy got there.

> When Timothy comes, see that you put him at ease among you, for he is doing the work of the Lord, as I am. So let no one despise him. Help him on his way in peace, that he may return to me, for I am expecting him with the brothers, 1 Corinthians 16:10–11.

Timothy personally attended to matters in many churches on behalf of Paul. Examples include Corinth, Thessalonica, and Ephesus. To get a better picture of the relationship between Paul and Timothy, required reading should cover the entire book of 2 Timothy. Paul opens up that very personal letter by calling Timothy his *beloved* (2 Timothy 1.2). It was very clear they had a strong relationship built on trust.

Paul and the Church at Philippi

A thorough reading of Philippians reveals a warm, loving relationship between Paul and this church. It is seen in verses like:

- 1.3–5: "I thank my God in all my remembrance of you, always in every prayer of mine for you all making my prayer with joy, **because of your partnership in the gospel from the first day until now.**"
- 1.7–8: "It is right for me to feel this way about you all, because **I hold you in my heart, for you are all partakers with me of grace**, both in my imprisonment and in the defense and confirmation of the gospel. For God is my witness, how **I yearn for you all with the affection of Christ Jesus.**"
- 4.14–20: "Yet it was kind of you to share my trouble. And you Philippians yourselves know that in the beginning of the gospel, when I left Macedonia, **no church entered into partnership with me in giving and receiving, except you only. Even in Thessalonica you sent me help for my needs once and again**. Not that I seek the gift, but I seek the fruit that increases to your credit. I have received full payment, and more. **I am well supplied, having received from Epaphroditus the gifts you sent, a fragrant offering, a sacrifice acceptable and pleasing to God. And my God will supply every need of yours according to his riches in glory in Christ Jesus.** To our God and Father be glory forever and ever. Amen."

It is clear from these excerpts that Paul dearly loved the Philippian church. The brothers and sisters truly cared for him. It is, the type of relationship that congregations and evangelists should strive to have with each other, as well as everyone within the local church family.

How to Build Trust Inside the Congregational Family

Now that we've read these two examples, let's focus on ten things[32] that everyone can do to build an atmosphere of trust here within our own spiritual family. When we do these things, not only will we be drawn closer together, but we will broaden our influence as well.

Lead by Example

Show how you trust others. If you are not actively pursuing other relationships and making yourself vulnerable, how can you ever expect others to trust you? In other words, *trust is earned.* If you make it a priority in your life, others will see it. *Therefore, confess your sins to one another and pray for one another, that you may be healed,* James 5.16a.

Practice Open Communication

Communication needs to be done in person. The true meaning of a message can get lost via text, email and sometimes even on the phone. Make sure you are both heard and understood by talking face to face.

Be Committed to Building Personal Relationships

Today's world thrives on the superficial. Today, you probably know more people than you ever have (think through social media, electronic media, etc.), but you may feel lonelier than you ever have. Life is better when we add real, meaningful, and close relationships to it.

When You Mess Up, Take Responsibility for your Actions

Don't place blame. Throwing other people "under the bus" is a sure way to dissolve any efforts you've made to build trust.

Keep your Promises

Let what you say be simply 'Yes' or 'No'; anything more than this comes from evil, Matthew 5.37. Keeping promises about "little things" are just as important as the "big things."

Keep Secrets

If someone speaks something to you in confidence, keep it that way. There is no quicker way to dissolve the trust someone else has in you than to divulge personal information that they do not want getting out. *Whoever covers an offense seeks love, but he who repeats a matter separates close friends,* Proverbs 17.9.

Don't Rush to Judgment

You might not understand why something is important to a brother or sister, but the fact that it is important is all that matters. Before you can trust, you must respect each other and your differences without judgment. *Know this, my beloved brothers: let every person be quick to hear, slow to speak, slow to anger;* James 1.19.

Be Forgiving

Trusting doesn't mean mistakes won't happen, and when they do, be forgiving. Holding on to past transgressions will only erode the trust in our relationships. We should feel the ability to make mistakes, and so should others within the group, without it being a constant source of contention. Letting go of the hurt, accepting the apology and moving on builds a trust based on truth and love. *Be kind to one another, tenderhearted, forgiving one another, as God in Christ forgave you,* Ephesians 4.32.

Disagree in Private

A public forum is never a place to voice a disagreement. If something your brother or sister is saying doesn't sit well with you, discuss it privately. Often disagreeing in front of other people can shame or humiliate the other person. This kind of behavior will damage your lines of communication and your trust factor. Waiting until a time you can meet in private offers the benefit of formulating your thoughts in a respectful way to encourage an honest and open discussion.

Be Supporting During the Good Times and the Bad

It is important in any relationship to be supportive of the other person. It is even more important to show that support when we are in a stage of building trust. If one person in the relationship doesn't feel that they can take a risk, make mistakes, or try new things without support, the relationship will falter.

Conclusion

Finally, give thought to these passages when thinking about building trust in relationships: Ephesians 4.25–32; Colossians 3.8–14; 1 Peter 3.8–9; 2 Corinthians 13.11. Active trust can be built when we all give careful attention to putting on the godly attitudes and lifestyle that comes with the new life in Christ.

For Thought and Reflection

1. Assessing your spiritual life presently, are the relationships you have with those in the spiritual family characterized by trust?

2. What are some things you can do to improve on strengthening the trust you have inside your relation-ships with brethren?

3. Describe Paul's relationship with Timothy. How was it built on trust?

4. What impresses you most about Paul's relationship with the Philippian church?

5. Is being vulnerable something hard for you? What are some things you can do to open up more to others? How will this help in building trust with others within the spiritual family?

6. How are communication efforts struggling in our modern age of electronic devices? How can we fix this?

7. Why is it important not to rush to judgment when dealing with other people?

8. How good are you at practicing forgiveness? What are some things you can do to improve?

9. How do passages like Ephesians 4.25–32; Colossians 3.8–14; 1 Peter 3.8–9; 2 Corinthians 13.11 help us build trust in our relationships?

Lesson 10

Bearing with One Other

Introduction

Can you think of someone who always seems to manage to *get under your skin?* Maybe it is their careless words and actions. Maybe it is a bad habit they possess. Or the person you are thinking of has recurring failures. Sometimes, people just do not get along, no matter how hard they try. Personality conflicts are very real and require a great deal of effort to get along.

How can we improve on the admonitions we find in Scripture?

Two Biblical Directives:

This lesson will primarily focus on these two texts:

> "I therefore, a prisoner for the Lord, urge you to walk in a manner worthy of the calling to which you have been called, with all humility and gentleness, with patience, bearing with one another in love, eager to maintain the unity of the Spirit in the bond of peace," Ephesians 4:1–3.

> "Put on then, as God's chosen ones, holy and beloved, compassionate hearts, kindness, humility, meekness, and patience, bearing with one another and, if one has a complaint against another, forgiving each other; as the Lord has forgiven you, so you also must forgive," Colossians 3:12–13.

What Does it Mean to Bear with One Another?

"Bearing" as found in Ephesians 4.2 and Colossians 3.13 is used in the sense of describing circumstances where a person has "to endure something unpleasant or difficult whether on one's own behalf or on behalf of someone else." In the Greek the word literally means to "endure, to put up with, or to suffer.[33]" Another dictionary defines it as "to hold oneself up against. To bear with, endure, forbear, or suffer."[34] Other Bible translations use words like *forbearing* (NRSV); *accepting each other* (NCV); *showing tolerance for* (NASB); and *making allowance for each other's faults* (NLT).

This really involves the ability to see further by moving with the end in view. It is the ability not to be swayed by the emotion of the moment.

How Do We Do It?

Develop Humility, Gentleness, and Patience

First, it requires humility, gentleness, and patience. Humility is the possession of a true assessment of oneself. Gentleness involves being considerate of the feelings of others. Patience is the ability to be slow to react when others annoy or anger you. We need to ask ourselves these questions:

1. What person is perfect?
2. How would I feel if I were that person?
3. How will my personal displeasure, frustration, or anger affect them or others?

Exercising humility, gentleness, and patience is the active practice of the fruit of the Spirit in Galatians 5.22–23 and is ultimately an expression of love.

A Desire to Forgive

Second, it may require a desire to forgive. Reread Colossians 3.13 and read Ephesians 4.32. Both passages turn us back to Jesus and the active practice of forgiveness.

A Commitment to Unity

Third, it involves a commitment to unity. When we examine the whole of the Ephesians passage—we understand that God is calling us to love the difficult people in life. It is part of walking worthily (4.1) and of maintaining the unity of the Spirit (4.3).

Accomplished by Love

Fourth, it is accomplished by love. Note especially Ephesians 4.2: Bearing with one another in love. This is the active practice of passages like:

> A new commandment I give to you, that you love one another: just as I have loved you, you also are to love one another. By this all people will know that you are my disciples, if you have love for one another, John 13:34–35.

> But I received mercy for this reason, that in me, as the foremost, Jesus Christ might display his perfect patience as an example to those who were to believe in him for eternal life, 1 Timothy 1:16.

> For if you forgive others their trespasses, your heavenly Father will also forgive you, Matthew 6:14.

What Might We Have to Bear?

In his blog, *Daily Encouragement*,[35] Stephen Weber listed several things to consider as we think about bearing with others. Who and what may we have to bear up under as we work with one another inside the local church family?[36]

- **People overcoming sin.** "We who are strong have an obligation to bear with the failings of the weak, and not to please ourselves." (Romans 15:1) See also 1 Thessalonians 5.14.

- **Differing convictions in areas of judgment.** See 1 Corinthians 8.

- **Emotional instability.** Different people react to different things in different ways. Not everyone is going to handle a situation in the exact same way you would.

- **Failed expectations.** How did Paul handle John Mark? See Acts 15.36-41 and 2 Timothy 4.11.

- **Differing understandings in the details of secondary matters of doctrine.** Unity is not uniformity. There should be an allowance for differences on the details, because not everyone is at the same place of understanding. e.g., Sunday evening communion; woman's covering; etc.

- **Practical matters like church money and business.** It has been said that we should never confuse taste or opinion with Biblical convictions.

- **Different expressions of spirituality.** Some are more emotional or demonstrative than others.

- **Political differences.** Think of the different apostles, who came from vastly different political backgrounds with equally diverging political views. This does not mean we should gloss over moral issues that creep into the political arena.

For Thought and Reflection

1. Read Ephesians 4.1–3 and Colossians 3.12–13. What about these passages impacts you most? How much work do you have to do in implementing these directives?

2. What does it mean to bear with one another in love?

3. How do humility, gentleness, and patience play a role in carrying out the command?

4. How can you become better at practicing forgiveness?

5. How is bearing with one another such an essential to unity?

6. How can you grow in the type of love Jesus calls for in John 13.34–35?

7. What might be our first temptation in handling the person who struggles with repetitive sin? How do we fight back?

8. How is overcoming differences in personal judgment accomplished?

9. How has politics come to affect church unity?

Lesson 11

Forgiving One Another

Introduction

I once read that those who work with animals in the wild say the only creatures' bears will allow to eat with them are skunks. Perhaps the reason is obvious. The cost of not living in peace with skunks is just too high! What a great principle, and one that all of us can learn from. There are many things in life that, if we give in to, will cost us far too much.

The Cost of Unforgiveness

For a moment, consider the cost of unforgiveness. It would certainly qualify. How much senseless pain has been perpetuated because individuals were unwilling to forgive? From marriages, to families, to nations, unforgiveness costs more than we should ever want to pay.

Are there relationships in your life that are struggling? Is something unforgiven creating distance with others and leading you to bitterness? No matter what caused the problem, creating a grudge and holding on to the pain is never worth creating a stink.

Counteracting an Unforgiving Spirit in Your Life

Remember God has called you to be compassionate

God seeks for your good by urging you to adopt kindness, humility, meekness, and patience in your life.

> Put on then, as God's chosen ones, holy and beloved, compassionate hearts, kindness, humility, meekness, and patience, bearing with one another and, if one has a complaint against another, forgiving each other; as the Lord has forgiven you, so you also must forgive, Colossians 3.12–13.

Will you make a commitment to bear with others and practice forgiveness? If the roles were reversed, what attitude would you desire to be directed toward you? See Matthew 7.12. Paul said, *be kind to one another, tenderhearted, forgiving one another, as God in Christ forgave you*, Ephesians 4.32.

Follow the Example of the Savior

Perhaps the secret of learning to forgive is most clearly seen in the sinless life of Jesus. His willingness to die on the cross for our sins cost Him everything.

Paul directed disciples to follow Jesus' example. *Forgive each other, as the Lord has forgiven you; as the Lord has forgiven you, so you must also forgive,* Colossians 3.14.

Remember Your Eternity Rests on Practicing Forgiveness

Jesus summed it up in the sermon on the mount: *For if you forgive others their trespasses, your heavenly Father will also forgive you, but if you do not forgive others their trespasses, neither will your Father forgive your trespasses,* Matthew 6.14–15. Will you step up to the challenge? You need to. The cost of unforgiveness is just too great!

How will you put this into practice?

Is your marriage struggling? Commit to practicing compassion, kindness, patience, and forgiveness.

Is your relationship with your children not where it should be? Find the time to communicate with them and begin again living out these virtues.

Are there strained friendships with those inside your spiritual family? Pray for help to let go and look ahead. Living in past hurt is never worth the displeasure it causes.

You can learn a lot from a bear. The price of not living in peace is just too high.[37]

For Thought and Reflection

1. How has unforgiveness cost you in your life? What have you learned from this?

2. How can you resist holding a grudge against someone?

3. Why is forgiveness so important:

- In marriage?

- In parenting?

- In the church?

- In all areas of life?

4. What are some things you can do to put Colossians 3.12–14 into practice more effectively?

5. How well do you do in following Jesus' admonition in Matthew 7.12? How can you improve?

6. What does Ephesians 4.32 teach you about forgiveness?

7. What does 1 Peter 2.22–25 teach us about forgiveness?

8. What is your first reaction after reading Matthew 6.14–15? How much improvement do you need to follow through?

9. What will you do this week to become more forgiving?

10. Why is forgiveness so essential to discipleship and fellowship?

Lesson 12

Submitting to One Another

Introduction

The second half of Ephesians is often referred to as the application section of the book. The doctrinal truths communicated in the first part of the book state matter-of-factly that the Christian has been saved by grace through faith, 2.8. Since this is true, we are to become an active participant in the body of believers, moved by thankfulness. This results in:

- Our walking worthily (4.1–3).
- Our commitment to spiritual growth (4.4–16).
- Living inside a new life that has been raised with Christ (4.17–24).
- Practicing self-control, integrity, encouraging speech, putting away wrath and malice, and moving with forgiveness (4.25–32).
- Becoming an imitator of God (5.1) that walks in love (5.2) and abstains from immorality (5.2–14).
- Applying wisdom and moving with understanding of the will of the Lord (5.15–17).

Never forget that God has taken you, who were dead, and has made you alive together with Christ, 2.4–7. He has made you, who once had no hope and were without God, a citizen with the saints and members of the household of God, 2.12,19. Because of these facts, why shouldn't we want to be who God has called us to be?

The General Responsibility of All Believers

Please take a moment and read Ephesians 5.18–21. First Paul speaks of being *filled with the Spirit*, 5.18. Imagine you are out on the water in a sailboat. As the wind blows, it fills the sail and carries you along in the direction it goes. When you have been born again, you are allowing yourself to be moved or called along in the direction the Spirit determines. The idea is that as time progresses, you become more and more like God.

Now, read 5.19–21. When your sails are filled with the Spirit, what will you do? Answer: your heart will be filled with joy, and you will not hesitate to praise God out loud. Our spiritual life should be full of personal expressions of joy to God. Notice also, you'll be full of thankfulness. You won't hesitate to say "thank you" to God through word and action. Your heart will be submissive and directed toward others.

Now, focus on Ephesians 5.21: *submitting to one another out of reverence for Christ*. What is the general responsibility of believers? Submission. The word literally means "to arrange under." It's a military term that meant to rank oneself under. In Paul's day, his readers would have understood the need to place oneself under someone else who has responsibility for you.

I think the idea of submission is moving farther and farther away inside our culture. The current generation of teens and young adults seems to have been coddled and is having difficulty transitioning into real life. Many can't seem to handle disagreement and require safe spaces where any dissent is silenced. Every generation of Americans since World War 2 seems to be more and more selfish. This seems very true today with many who seem to just focus on self-glorification and domination of the space around them with their own plans and opinions.

This is not what is communicated in Ephesians 5. The idea is that if you reverence Jesus, you will have the desire to honor and please Him. This means you will be committed to becoming a submissive person who is not dominating, self-willed, or attached to your own agenda.

The General Principle of Submission

When you read of the expectations surrounding unity in Philippians 1.27—2.2, 1 Corinthians 1.10–12, or Ephesians 4.1–3, how do you enact them? How can people get along so completely? The answer is found in Philippians 2.3–4. These two verses are the heart of submission. They are humility in action. This is what is produced as we allow the Spirit to fill our spiritual sail and move us along on the path to becoming more like God.

Jesus lived this out. In Philippians 2.5–8, Paul spells out the greatest illustration of submission.

- 2.5—it begins in the heart.
- 2.6–8a—it is revealed through humility.
- 2.8b—it responds in obedience.
- 2.9—it results in exaltation.

Next, submission is spoken of in 1 Peter 2.13—3.12. There Peter discusses submission in public life (2.15–17); in work relationships (2.18–20); Jesus (2.21–25); wives (3.1–6); husbands (3.7); and one to another (3.18–12.)

Submission is seen in the broad command of 1 Corinthians 16.15b–16.

Submission needs to be seen in how we respond to our leaders, Hebrews 13.17; 1 Peter 5.5.

It has been said that it is the submissive attitude that makes the Christian life work. It's foundational to everything. Everyone submits at some level. Apart from it, dysfunction, and chaos reigns.

For Thought and Reflection

1. What does it mean to be filled with the Spirit?

2. What are three results of being filled with the Spirit as found in Ephesians 5.19–21?

    a.

    b.

    c.

3. What does *submission* mean? Why do you think Americans have such a hard time practicing submission? How does this creep into the church? Christianity? One's own personal spiritual life?

4. Can we refuse to submit to others and still reverence Jesus? Why/Why Not?

5. What two verses might be called the heart of submission?

6. Who serves as the best example of submission? How does Philippians 2.6–8 prove this?

7. What does submission lead to? (Philippians 2.9)

8. What did Peter teach about submission? (1 Peter 2.13–3.12)

9. Why must we submit to our congregational leaders? (Hebrews 13.17; 1 Peter 5.5)

10. How does submission make the Christian life work?

11. What happens when submission is not practiced?

Lesson 13

Loving One Another

Introduction

If you really fulfill the royal law according to the Scripture, "You shall love your neighbor as yourself," you are doing well, James 2.8.

Love is the basis for every expectation found in Christianity. We demonstrate our love for God by serving others with sacrificial love. *This is my commandment, that you love one another as I have loved you,* John 15.12.

In the final days of His ministry, Jesus reinforced this teaching in Matthew 22.37–40: *And he said to him, "You shall love the Lord your God with all your heart and with all your soul and with all your mind. This is the great and first commandment. And a second is like it: You shall love your neighbor as yourself. On these two commandments depend all the Law and the Prophets."*

We need to treat all people as we would want to be treated, Matthew 7.12.

Who do you take into greater consideration? Others? Or yourself?

How Can You Fulfill the Royal Law?

Listen

Look for someone who may be having a bad day and needs someone to talk to. Sometimes we need to do less talking and just open our ears.

Commit to serving someone else

You can do this by helping, encouraging, and giving of yourself. It is one thing to say you care. Do others know how much you care by the deeds you do? See 1 John 3.17–18.

Call someone or send a card

Others inside your local congregation may be struggling with an illness or coping with a spiritual problem. It may seem like a small thing, but the encouragement and loved expressed are hard to measure.

Visit an elderly brother or sister

Let them know you are interested in their life.

Find a young person inside your spiritual family…

that you can mentor.

Pray for your spiritual family

Name specific brothers and sisters that enter your mind. Thank God for their example, ask for His assistance in their spiritual life, and pray for their good.

Pray for your enemies

Pray for those who spitefully denigrate you. You never know how God will go to work in what seems like an impossible situation.

Conclusion

This is Christianity in action. It is the application of 1 John 3.17–19: *But if anyone has the world's goods and sees his brother in need, yet closes his heart against him, how does God's love abide in him? Little children, let us not love in word or talk but in deed and in truth. By this we shall know that we are of the truth and reassure our heart before him.*

Fulfill the royal law and magnify Christ today by the way you reach out to someone.

For Thought and Reflection

1. What is the royal law of Scripture?

2. How do we demonstrate our love for God?

3. How do we keep the first great commandment? (Matthew 22.40)

4. How can you improve in treating other people the way you want to be treated?

5. Would you describe yourself as a good listener? How can you improve?

6. How do others inside the family know you care?

7. Who is someone you can help mentor?

8. Who are some inside the spiritual family that you can pray for?

9. How does the teaching of 1 John 3.17–19 apply to today's lesson?

10. What is the best way for other people to see that you are a Christian? Explain.

Endnotes

1 Strong, James. *A Concise Dictionary of the Words in the Greek Testament and The Hebrew Bible*. Bellingham, WA: Logos Bible Software, 2009.

2 Arndt, William, Frederick W. Danker, and Walter Bauer. *A Greek-English Lexicon of the New Testament and Other Early Christian Literature*. Chicago: University of Chicago Press, 2000.

3 Freedman, David Noel, Gary A. Herion, David F. Graf, John David Pleins, and Astrid B. Beck, eds. *The Anchor Yale Bible Dictionary*. New York: Doubleday, 1992.

4 Richards, Daniel. *Ten Simple Ways to Build Each Other Up*. Adapted and retrieved 05/27/2017 from http://www.becomingminimalist.com/ten-simple-ways-to-build-each-other-up/

5 Wellman, Jack. *What Does Exhortation Mean? A Biblical Definition of Exhortation*. No Pages. 6/3/2017. http://www.patheos.com/blogs/christiancrier/2015/08/15/what-does-exhortation-mean-a-biblical-definition-of-exhortation/, 2015.

6 Arndt, William, Frederick W. Danker, and Walter Bauer. *A Greek-English Lexicon of the New Testament and Other Early Christian Literature*. Chicago: University of Chicago Press, 2000.

7 Minor, Eugene. *An Exegetical Summary of 2 Timothy*. 2nd ed. Dallas, TX: SIL International, 2008.

8 Moss, C. Michael. *1, 2 Timothy & Titus*. The College Press NIV Commentary. Joplin, MO: College Press, 1994.

9 Kittel, Gerhard, Geoffrey W. Bromiley, and Gerhard Friedrich, eds. *Theological Dictionary of the New Testament*. Grand Rapids, MI: Eerdmans, 1964–.

10 MacArthur, John. *Marks of the Faithful Preacher, Part 2*. No pages. 6/3/2017. https://www.gty.org/library/sermons-library/55-21/marks-of-the-faithful-preacher-part-2, 1988.

11 Pease, Glenn. *The Gift of Exhortation*. No Pages. 6/3/2017. https://soundfaith.com/sermons/125166-the-gift-of-exhortation, 2014.

12 Elton Trueblood. Quoted in the Peace article.

13 Pease.

14   Louw, Johannes P., and Eugene Albert Nida. *Greek-English Lexicon of the New Testament: Based on Semantic Domains.* New York: United Bible Societies, 1996.

15   The first main meaning is "weak," or "weakness," or "to be weak," originally in the physical sense. In the NT the words are hardly ever used of purely physical weakness, but frequently in the comprehensive sense of the whole man. There is also a "weakness which must be overcome." This is a weakness of religious and moral condition. More precisely these are the weak in faith, as in Romans 4.19; 5.6; 14.1–2, 21; 1 Corinthians 8.9, 11–12. See Stählin, Gustav. "Ἀσθενής, Ἀσθένεια, Ἀσθενέω, Ἀσθένημα." Edited by Gerhard Kittel, Geoffrey W. Bromiley, and Gerhard Friedrich. *Theological Dictionary of the New Testament.* Grand Rapids, MI: Eerdmans, 1964–.

16   MacArthur, John. *The Power of Righteous Praying, James 5.13–18.* Grace to You. No Pages. 6/6/2017 http://www.gty.org, 1987.

17   The Lexham Analytical Lexicon to the Greek New Testament. Logos Bible Software, 2011.

18   Sophocles, E. A. *Greek Lexicon of the Roman and Byzantine Periods (From B. C. 146 to A. D. 1100).* New York: Charles Scribner's Sons, 1900.

19   Walton Weaver: *Let's Talk about Prayer.*

20   Albert Barnes.

21   Cottrell, Jack. Romans. Vol. 2. *The College Press NIV Commentary.* Joplin, MO: College Press Pub. Co., 1996.

22   MacArthur, John. *Romans.* logos.com. Bellingham, WA, 1991.

23   Kittel, Gerhard, Geoffrey W. Bromiley, and Gerhard Friedrich, eds. "Εὐπροσωπέω." *Theological Dictionary of the New Testament.* Grand Rapids, MI: Eerdmans, 1964–.

24   Simeon, Charles. *Horae Homileticae: Romans.* Vol. 15. London: Holdsworth and Ball, 1833.

25   Simeon.

26   Simeon.

27   Garrett, Linda. "Love Divided Against Itself?" *Bible Study Magazine.* Page 6. Volume 9, No. 5, July/August 2017.

28   Strong, James. *A Concise Dictionary of the Words in the Greek Testament and The Hebrew Bible.* Bellingham, WA: Logos Bible Software, 2009.

29 Arndt, William, Frederick W. Danker, and Walter Bauer. *A Greek-English Lexicon of the New Testament and Other Early Christian Literature.* Chicago: University of Chicago Press, 2000.

30 See also Paul's comments regarding the Philippian church financial support of his ministry in Philippians 4.10–20.

31 The "if" clauses turn out not to express supposition, but presupposition, and should therefore be translated something closer to "since there is …"; and the apodosis, instead of expressing the "then" side of a supposition, takes the form of an imperative based on the presuppositions. See Fee, Gordon D. *Paul's Letter to the Philippians. The New International Commentary on the New Testament.* Grand Rapids, MI: Wm.B. Eerdmans Publishing Co., 1995.

32 See "10 Ways to Build Trust in Relationships." Online: https://www.powerofpositivity.com/10-ways-to-build-trust-in-a-relationship/

33 Strong, James. *A Concise Dictionary of the Words in the Greek Testament and The Hebrew Bible.* Bellingham, WA: Logos Bible Software, 2009.

34 Horst, Johannes. "Μακροθυμία, Μακροθυμέω, Μακρόθυμος, Μακροθύμως." Edited by Gerhard Kittel, Geoffrey W. Bromiley, and Gerhard Friedrich. *Theological Dictionary of the New Testament.* Grand Rapids, MI: Eerdmans, 1964–.

35 Weber, Stephen. "Bearing With One Another." No Pages. 7/12/2017. http://dailyencouragement.net

36 I have changed the wording of several of Weber's points in bold as well as the remarks afterward.

37 Francis Anfuso "Bears and Skunks." Retrieved 08/13/2013 from http://www.francisanfuso.com/klove-features/klove-radio-features-february-2013/

www.ingramcontent.com/pod-product-compliance
Lightning Source LLC
Chambersburg PA
CBHW060424050426
42449CB00009B/2122